Invasives

poems by

Emily Kingery

Finishing Line Press
Georgetown, Kentucky

Invasives

Copyright © 2023 by Emily Kingery
ISBN 979-8-88838-144-1 First Edition
All rights reserved under International and Pan-American Copyright Conventions. No part of this book may be reproduced in any manner whatsoever without written permission from the publisher, except in the case of brief quotations embodied in critical articles and reviews.

ACKNOWLEDGMENTS

I am grateful to the editors of the following journals, in which these poems, sometimes under different titles or in earlier versions, first appeared:

GASHER Journal: "Growing Season" and "Marshmallow Test"
High Shelf Press: "Reunion"
Painted Bride Quarterly: "Dirtbag Wilderness"
Quercus: "Bright Girls" and "The Light of Fragile Things"
Sidereal Magazine: "Tricks"
Small Orange Journal: "Porch Light"

The poem "Toxicity" borrows lyrics from the song of the same name by System of a Down.

Publisher: Leah Huete de Maines
Editor: Christen Kincaid
Cover Art and Design: Lisa Huntsha
Author Photo: Emily Kingery

Order online: www.finishinglinepress.com
also available on amazon.com

Author inquiries and mail orders:
Finishing Line Press
PO Box 1626
Georgetown, Kentucky 40324
USA

Table of Contents

Musk Thistle 1

The Basement 2

Game Theory 3

The Black Sleep 4

Toxicity 5

Tricks 6

Dirtbag Wilderness 7

Bright Girls 10

July 11

Origin Story 12

Fusion 13

The Blue House 14

Sentence 15

April 16

Logic Problem 17

Growing Season 18

Recursion 19

Bargain 20

Hound 21

Marshmallow Test 22

Porch Light 23

On Another's Sorrow 24

Ritual 25

Reunion 26

The Light of Fragile Things 28

Waste 29

Resurrection 31

The Birdbath 32

Toxicology 33

For Ben
(1982-2021)

Musk Thistle

In the years before the Internet, there was no good way
to ask what makes a flower a weed. Each season, we

drooped in men's heavy gloves. We stood in pastures
with open grocery bags for gathering, watched how

the executioners wrenched their heads in the shears.
The cows, we were told, would eat the stems and

leaves and the spines would scrape through them, grate
blood from their innards to the soil. We were told it was

ours to control the pain by setting the blooms on fire.
When the wireless signal reached our homes, we set

the heads as our backgrounds. We Googled *plumes* and
bracts and enough Latin to raise demons and we forgot

about cows, forgot to clear our histories. Ads sprang up.
We unsubscribed, but the seeds could keep in the soil

for a decade, longer. They could be so hard to control.

The Basement

We won't say what we buried without killing:
the house of blankets, the plastic keys. He was

the one I called *my friend* at recess, then shut
my eyes as boys spun the chains of my swing

and let go. We were married in the basement,
before or after my Barbies enacted scenes

from movies I couldn't have watched. Before
or after they were strewn in my bedroom,

limbs and breasts hard and blank and I blamed
my playdates. Each time the swing untwisted,

it felt good to spin, and the smell of his shirt
was good: a clothesline, a lawn just cut. And

it was good of him to vow that he would
cherish me. And build a home, if I obeyed.

Game Theory

I am becoming a parakeet, or afraid
I am. Turning green of limes, of gleaming
nails. Of book-fair posters of green-eyed
cats. A cat appears and I sprout wings. He
lights my breast in a tractor beam and I
lie still. We share the room. We sleep in
artificial dark. *I dare you,* says the cat
behind ponies with combs in their manes.
I thrill for him. I recognize my green in him.
He licks my wires. Sucks pink from me into
his neon maw while the bedroom TV glows
with slime. It gushes from the set, crashes
heads of losing children. They choke out
laughs in octaves. They go home poor.

The Black Sleep

When they caught me with cigarettes, the girls
at the sleepover said to confess, so I confessed

my lust for Indiana Jones. The temple was mine,
my VHS gospel: a brainless girl, sequined with

centipedes winding in the shadows of her flesh,
her lover in torch light turned murderous from

a drink. I adored his devotion to hearts: the clutch
and twist as to a combination lock. I worshipped

and they returned laden with popcorn and Coke.
They shrieked straight through, thought I was sick,

went to sleep in their hot-pink lies. When my father
trashed my cigarettes and drove me away, I rewound,

dreamed adult dreams of descent into ceremony.
The spectacle was everything and nothing I had

would return men to their senses, men who called me
sweetheart. I would let any of them take me home.

Toxicity

He hangs up, and I think of the skip of CDs
in his car, the perfume of clove cigarettes

I bought to taste his breath when he was
never close. The Everclear he poured, toasting

to us when proximity made an *us*, the song
on a loop in his room, asking, *How do you own*

disorder? I wandered our one-stoplight town
until he drove by, and we drove away until

the policemen crawled, not for us but for
the music. The first time, I opened the door

and he gripped my hand, held it still through
How do you own disorder? He reached behind

for the stems of baby's breath discarded from
someone's bouquet. I accepted the cellophane

like a child in awe. What if they grew in my arms,
showed him how easily he could give to me?

Tricks

They offer me apples from their backpacks, but I have read
enough of Genesis not to be duped, drunk enough Hydroxycut

that I am finally on fire. I hear the apples split like bones
in their heads. They crack open books, copy me and scrub out

their mistakes with erasers, soft and pink and they never
think to eat them. They are not to be loved, they who measure

in facts, they who have no fondness for the crest of an ilium
or rib under a boyfriend's palm, they whose straps stay put

where no thumbs can glide under. Adams grow hungry,
they tire of God and their animals and vanish like scarves

up a sleeve. They get expelled, find trees that are ready to drop
and shake down to their ankles a lineage. They are filthy

with apples without me. They offer, but I have read enough
to know I am half-gone already. I have cut enough flesh

that when the crosscut saw is flourished in the garden
for the final trick, my body will disappear on its own.

Dirtbag Wilderness

Our dirtbags, our dirtbags
were medicine men.

They spoke as oracles,
capped bottles, skated

razorblades across
the glass of pictures.

It's just like shoveling snow,
laughed our dirtbags

as they unburied
their parents' faces.

Like raking leaves,
want to try?

We watched their hands
swap bills, our eyes

the wrong kind of wild.
Our dirtbags laughed:

You can sit with us
while we finish.

This was intimacy:
our sitting, their finishing.

We laughed; we returned
frames to their shelves.

We bought shadows dark
and lip stains darker. *Darker,*

said our dirtbags, damp
on basement couches.

We envied in secret
the laughs of bright girls,

high as their hair
pinned in hard, slick curls.

They spun like acrobats
in the high school gym,

strobing in glitz
we were disallowed.

Bitches, spat our dirtbags,
skanks, whichever

words coaxed our laughter.
We swallowed them

like expectorant
and laughed in wet coughs

under canopies
of parking lot trees,

our arms crossed as though
coffined already.

We rolled in our dirtbags' scent
like hunting dogs,

napped in stuffy rooms
as their hands, their hands

blessed guns, made backpacks
heavy with Ziploc holy.

It's all good, laughed our dirtbags.
Our hips, our ponytails

swayed easy as leaves.
By summer, our dirtbags

wore sly, deep pockets,
weighed powders,

held capsules to the light
under a jeweler's loupe.

The car windows glided,
phones lit up like lightning

bugs on the shoulders
of gravel roads. Such soft light,

light of vigils, light the yellow
of a forgiven bruise.

We rode to neighboring towns
of missing teeth and needles.

We cried in bathrooms
far from home. We were home

when we laughed, when we laughed
we laughed Everclear vomit.

But our dirtbags, our dirtbags
let us sit while they finished,

and their hands were warm
as stones pressing us to sleep.

Bright Girls

We had visions more necessary than eyes.
We dressed up our names for funerals
and piled plenty of dirt on the flowers.

We spent our summers not begging
for forgiveness, but pinching apart
our cuts to keep them bright. At parties,

we flinched like lambs in brambles,
shook our hair to scatter out thorns.
We cried over them, ceremoniously.

Other girls said *starving after*. They
pushed our thorns into piles at the sink
and, sneering, called them pins.

We made our meals of coke, holding in
like balloons. Whole birds appeared
less to us than bones in a wing.

Where is my, we took turns wailing.
We thought of *mother, pride,* but those
were easy words, too plain.

We let the vowels of *where is my*
curve alone in our mouths
like coming, or significance.

We repeated them like dead first loves.
We swapped our lives for theirs because
that is what it was to believe,

and no one said it would make orphans of us all,
and no one said it didn't count as communion,
that vision is not eating, but eating is,

that *oh, Christ* is a phrase for girls
who dawdle in long aisles of bread,
waiting to be asked if they are lost.

July

The party cake
peeled like skin

in fire. Behind you,
the spreading

bruise of sky, trees
shuddering and

a hover
where insects

had drawn
blood as you took me

home. Fireflies
flared from the corn

where children
wove in, unafraid

to lose the way
back. They would

bloom rashes
on their limbs,

let the mystery
of skin

unfurl
until it vanished.

Origin Story

We name a place we pretend we'll visit
for Christmas, let it tumble out

too hot to swallow and raise our drinks
with so much ice they punch us

when we tilt back, make our teeth shine
like weapons under policemen's lights.

Fusion

When I look in mirrors, I see two men
instead of me. The first is the bartender
who tongued my ear: *Your scar is sexy.*

I said, *It's surgical.* He gripped my clothes,
said, *You need a new story* and gave me one
while girls held other girls' hair back.

I conjured new stories: feral cats,
knife fights in alleys where guns are drawn.
My hair fell thick. I returned to the bar

to tell the second a story. I said *magical*
then, like the lies were twins sharing skin.

The Blue House

You confessed your father hit you,
slid his belt from the loops

to teach you. Said it didn't hurt you
to tell me, said it was your first time

drawing up the secret. I drank it:
first time, almost true. I thought

of belts I knew, secrets no more than
hands changing color in cold, stories

of gloves left in cars and their owners
too foolish to go back. You parked

two blocks away from streetlights
in the lot where a father had once

painted the house blue, barking
obscenities at children. I changed

the story of the mice, said they fled
when the house was razed. I said

I released them to the grass at night,
I didn't believe in traps. I may as well have

said *first time*. I might have imagined more
distance for the mice, enough for them

to forget the way back. I think of them, dead
in their nests in the rubble. I think of them

and you, eyes wet with stories. Sometimes
of families, of all that wasted paint.

Sentence

Before prison, time matters
how a sermon matters

to a boy who puts gum
in your hair. You guess

how much you have left
before trying lemon oil.

You use kitchen scissors
the morning after, walk

to school with your hair
and breath so desperate

the boy can't love you,
not like that. And when

you're not that girl,
you're no one else, taking

his only phone call, still
in thrall of stories pulled

like threats through teeth,
just so. Just right to land

in his mother's hands,
but he wads them

to your scalp. To
no other girl but you.

April

I am in my living room
watching Waco footage,

or in my homeroom
when a building explodes

in Oklahoma. The blazes
and aviator glasses

in the Jesus-portraits
stay, and the fireman

with the dead infant
has never looked up

from his magazine and
I have never grown up

from the stardom of
lonely men who say

they have principle and
I don't argue. Who argues

with men who undress you
the way summer does

to spring, who fool you into
believing they're not

just any outlaw men
named for Biblical men

plotting violent exits
and inviting you to join?

Logic Problem

He didn't take my life, and he didn't
drink all the milk. I was wrong to say it
that time. Many times wrong to say *all*.

It reminds me, the milk, of that logic
problem: one knight, one knave, a door
or a bridge. All you have to do is ask

the right question. Do you remember?
Trick question. That's not how it was,
you bitch. I find myself on bridges

listening to the river over rocks and
bottle glass. Cornfields seem empty,
but they're flush with crows, some

women too used to put in graves, mice
and cats on the prowl from quiet barns.
I could have shaken out the milk.

I could have done more, done right
by those animals. They have to kill
if you don't feed them. Even if you do.

Growing Season

Your wife grows tomatoes in your yard and they are
perfect. They are round like clown noses for the baby
to grab and they shine like ornaments she will learn
to hook and hang in time. There are enough tomatoes
for your wife to share with the town we live in, to leave
blanketed in tea towels on the porches of women
who used to be my neighbors, too. Your wife borrows
clothespins to hang your bed linen when she runs out
after the diapers. You did not tell her the story of the dog
whose hip broke in late-stage cancer, whose diapers
I helped your mother change. When the dog died,
you said it felt like losing a son. You never had a son.
Your wife does not need to know this to love you, and
she does not need to know we asked you to lift the dog
and you fled the kitchen in disgust. She does not need
to know you tore a light from the ceiling and smashed
it on the floor. She does not need to think of me at all
crawling in search of glass. She runs her fingers over
the vines in the garden and fills a basket while the baby
sleeps. You named the baby together. The neighbors
brought loaves of zucchini bread tied in cellophane
and pink ribbon. They say she has her father's smile,
his eyes, his brain. When she babbles, she says *Daddy*
as if she loves you. When your wife repeats it, coaxing her
to say it, she does not need for any of it to be true.

Recursion

I happen to meet him on the sidewalk,
sometimes in the grocery store

testing ripeness and evaluating dates
on cartons. Of course, we sleep together,

or we don't. Mostly there is the rush
of abandoning our shopping carts,

then the inelegant coda in which
I press my face to his shirt.

The dream is an easy one, but I am not
without problems. There is still

the grocery list in the morning, still
the conviction his daughter is my own.

Bargain

When I walk it down the aisle
held lightly on my hip, everyone

smiles at me, an important woman
with somewhere to go

who cannot possibly eat so much
without help. I am cute

to the clerk who scans the bag,
size of a sleepover pillow.

When I carry it to my car,
old men chuckle and wave

for me to cross. I am a mother
duck with a single duckling,

I am on my way to a party
where I will bring

honor to my foremothers.
Tenderly, I will peel open

the bag, set it snug in a cradle
of tiny Crock-Pots,

and wipe down the table
when it's over, when

everyone is in front of the TV,
sleeping like the children

I am forgiven for not bringing
into this world.

Hound

A pair of ducks lies in the dark
between our houses. We snap
pictures and the dog pulls hard
at his leash, hunting or pretending.
Either way, alive. It rains all May and
floods the river, and the dog whines
each night a storm comes through,
scared of thunder. I dread his howl,
the shake of jowls when he runs
straight to me. But I don't move.
I let him lay his head in my lap.

Marshmallow Test

It turns dark at the backyard barbecue
and the lawn chairs collapse. Dark beer
sputters on our shorts and shoes and
wine has purpled all the towels inside.
The men in their forties are balancing
mid-priced liquor on their foreheads
and the women are keeping score. I am
dizzy and charring all the marshmallows.
Who is he? they say, because I am laughing,
because I am drunk and my heart is good
as a bubble on the tongue or a hydrangea
shaking its petals to the dark of the yard.
I think of you opening the door in the hall
when I am too drunk to say your name but
awake enough to say *marry me.* How you
spread your hand in my hair, how we tangle
like tree roots and you answer, *tomorrow.*
You slide to the fire. You fill and refill a cup
while I spear at sugar, unhanded for good.

Porch Light

I was the first to visit in remission, to hold still
his hand until the music dwindled to a low

insect whine. Carnations and stargazer lilies
lay still throughout the house, their petals

the dark bruises of junkies, their tongues
a thousand of his when he let fall to his porch

a mouthful of bile and it shimmered there
under the light. His quiet said, *I owe you*

nothing, and I did nothing, as if to say
I know, or *I forgive you,* or *soon you will*

know the mystery of my heart, et cetera.
Each word an arrow sharpened toward

no mystery. Each a pang of knowing
the yearning to hear my name in his mouth

was a loud, dogged thing. A hunger
of a furnace, old and empty of coal.

On Another's Sorrow

I tongued him like a toothache for a decade, the lover
of suicidal women. I tongued his words to pearls.

And the kid from church who swung mice by their tails,
wound up and pitched them at the walls of his barn,

learned the trick from his brothers. When our church
held a Seder to teach us seriousness, he stayed polite

through the meal. He read the script: *Why is this night
different from all other nights?* It was less a question

than a trap. That boy in black jeans, black coat was
so out of my reach I loved him. When he lined up cups

of salt water to demonstrate Jell-O shots, I didn't tell.
I asked what he had suffered to drink so many tears.

Ritual

I do it every spring: get loaded, make lists
of what else is loaded. Baked potatoes,
washing machines, Oldsmobile trucks
heading west to Beverly Hills.

Drunks and billionaires, drunk billionaires.
Emily Dickinson guarding her Master
on an eiderdown pillow at nightfall.
I load and bang out questions

on the phone and you say you will not
outlive me. I am loaded as bases
at the bottom of the ninth, weeping
for daffodils slumping low under

April snow. I am Vesuvian, ready
for the rise and set of your number
until you have answers for me, answers
or the gin runs out. (It always runs out.)

Reunion

We enter the cemetery to touch
the illegible names on stones,

quiet and damp to our skin
as cellars, even now, when

the brittle August grass
breaks under us like cereal.

Oak branches snap as squirrels
leap in fright, in play; teenagers

swerve their parents' cars to the edges
where there are no plots.

We guess they stash drugs in the glove boxes,
undress each other, and we are right

without knowing if we are.
Decades have slipped from our lives

since we did the same, though it's wrong
to say we are in mourning, even if

we are. I have imagined the two
of your exes who died by suicide

are the air wicking away our sweat,
are the birds the size of gargoyles

calling out for each other in the
voices of cats. *That says something*

about us, you say, but you don't say
what I want. When high beams swoop

our path, they light animals preying
on each other. We feel afraid

of ourselves. We are never so ready
to run or to maul a pitiful body down

to bone, never ready. I know
what I want. I want what animals want

when they are threatened, when the light
has been dissolved. I am willing your mouth

to say, *We will,* to complete the sentence
with flesh, with impulse, with car windows

clouded with breath instead of weather.
The insects are violent in our ears.

You say if the gates are shut when we leave,
we will go right through them, like ghosts.

The Light of Fragile Things

Snow collects where you will soon
disappear to a name, a footprint filling.
You will close your eyes, pretend
we have been a lesson in color

and light: the light the flashbulb leaves
in our eyelids when it snaps, the light
that stays as overexposures: my hands
two slick-feathered starlings, blots

circling over white that widens.
Before you wake, I turn the blinds,
envying how slats of light bend
from my window to your ribs.

Waste

The boys sell me liquor, value-sized bottles
of pills. They turn to rattles in their hands.

We are separated by glass and the numbers
of two centuries, and I know they know

I am safe. They flirt with me, make me
laugh, ask for my license. I give it to them.

They will come to work the next day having
slept off a fantasy. One, who cares which,

will key the door to my building and it will be
you in your snow-shouldered coat. Your walk

down every sidewalk and hall, criminally long
and sure. *Always*, I slurred to your chest

in half-buttoned clothes, *always* a tombstone
I carved with my tongue. It needs me still

to bring clusters of pink I insist I love
but let rot in the moss of your bed. I pour

straight down my throat, too tired to hold
two things. It isn't true you were a boy

with a switch, whipping grass to scare
animals for sport, but that's the dream

I deserve. It is another *always*, erasing
one night at a time how you drank from

jars when the jelly or brine was gone and
the disposal, doglike, throated food

you would not finish. How you swung
my hand in yours like a plaything, tearing

me like cloth, hollowing my mind
for a body that would die like light.

Resurrection

I once believed you stole them
from our neighbors' flowerbeds

instead of graves. Blood-knuckled, dirt
in your nails: just the price of roses

after dark. I think, now, of all that
I would write if only I could stop

writing about flowers. I keep
a cupboard of vases for nothing, just

push them in your dirt. Strangers notice,
believe someone is stealing from you.

Some say you deserve it and I don't
know what I believe. In winter, I watch

men set out more wreaths than any
man can carry. Still, you might

bring one to my door, shake needles
from your coat and skin and hold me

still for love of poison. You could
smudge my hand with your cold mouth.

The Birdbath

When his daughter asks if we were in love,
I tell her about the birdbath. It was concrete,
cool under maple shade. If I tipped it enough,
it spilled out hose water and became a step
to the nearest limb. When I climbed the tree,
I didn't climb it. I stepped into it and sat there
with a book, like I had seen a girl my age do
in a book I once had read. I watched the leaves
shake patterns of light on the lawn and prayed
for no insects, since no insects plagued the girl
in the book. I imagined the neighbor boys spied
from their houses and whispered *how pretty* and
how brave, the fond way deceivers imagine. I fell
out of the dream when the birdbath fell, when
the only way down was to jump. It exposed
anthills, shimmering and threatened, and I
tell her anyone could have seen, but he
walked the neighborhood all summer. He
held a magnifying glass in his hand.

Toxicology

She could see for herself who I was
in the hometown pictures: the shot of
my swimsuit and duck-down hair, a popsicle
crying down my fist. I was afraid of splashing,

so I stood in the bucket set out for washing
our feet before the pool, and I just watched
the grass clippings. Sometimes I stared at
the heads of Queen Anne's lace in the yard

and traced the patterns with my fingers.
It was dangerous, knowing what we know
about lookalikes, how invasive species will
blister and scar your arms, even blind you

for life. I said I gathered them into bouquets
and walked around the block like a bride
with no husband. She said my story was sad,
that she couldn't tell if I was the same girl.

She couldn't tell. I swear, she couldn't.

Emily Kingery is an English professor at St. Ambrose University and the author of *Invasives* (Finishing Line Press, 2023), a semi-finalist in the New Women's Voices Series. Her work appears widely in journals, including *Birdcoat Quarterly, Blood Orange Review, GASHER, The Madison Review, Midwest Review, New Ohio Review, Painted Bride Quarterly, Raleigh Review,* and *Sidereal,* among others. She was a finalist for the 2022 Laureate Prize for full-length poetry manuscripts and has been a chapbook finalist at Harbor Editions and Thirty West Publishing House, as well as the recipient of honors and awards in both poetry and prose at *Eastern Iowa Review, Iron Horse Literary Review, Midway Journal, Nimrod International Journal, Quarter After Eight,* and *Small Orange Journal.* She serves on the Board of Directors at the Midwest Writing Center (mwcqc.org), a non-profit supporting writers in the Illinois-Iowa Quad Cities community. You can read more of her work at emilykingery.com.

www.ingramcontent.com/pod-product-compliance
Lightning Source LLC
Chambersburg PA
CBHW022123090426
42743CB00008B/976